MW00960851

The Beauty of a Slow Death

Understanding the Meaning of Acceptance, Living and Fading into Peace

3/25/2012

Author Michele DeMeo
Edited by Julie E. Williamson

Have a Fabulous life

Table of Contents

Foreword

Every now and then, if we're lucky, we come across a person whose unique qualities transform us in ways we never imagined. In knowing this individual, our beliefs are shaken, our dreams are awakened, and our burdens are somehow lifted. And in the process, our lives are changed forever. For me, that person is Michele DeMeo.

We first met in 2008 – before her being diagnosed with amyotrophic lateral sclerosis (ALS). I was editor for a healthcare association that represented her profession, and she contacted me to discuss the possibility of writing an article for the association's publication. From that first phone call, I knew I'd found someone special – a person with a passion for her profession, a kind, generous spirit, and a sincere desire to use her knowledge to help others. That day, she not only became my newest columnist, but also my dear friend and mentor.

While Michele's professional gifts were readily apparent, I quickly learned that she had so much more to teach – about life and, even more importantly, about living well, regardless of the circumstances...even when facing death.

No question, in her 38 years, she has truly lived. She has shared that, in some ways, her life really began when she was diagnosed with a terminal illness. Despite a bleak prognosis and a body that was betraying her, she picked herself up, dusted herself off and started putting her next goals into action. Writing and publishing this book was one of them.

Some might question why a person nearing the end of their life would even consider spending their days penning a book. But for Michele, putting her experience into writing was not just a cathartic escape, but rather a way to help others learn to live in a more deliberate, thoughtful and meaningful way.

Michele stresses that our inevitable passing (and even the days leading up to it) is not to be feared. Instead, she points out, the only thing scary about dying is not living our days, however many we have left, to their fullest.

This book is brief, yet its powerful message will surely endure. Michele's hope: that her personal journey and ability to live fully, even in the presence of a devastating diagnosis, will help others set aside their fears and negativity and seek a better, more fulfilling life...*right now*. What a wonderful legacy.

Being asked to edit my friend's book has been an incredible honor and making my way through her beautiful story -- line by line and word by word -- has been a gift I will forever cherish. As you read Michele's story, delve into her journey and begin exploring how you, too, can find acceptance, peace and outright joy in even the darkest of times, I believe you will feel the same.

~ Julie E. Williamson, writer, editor, friend

Introduction

Not all deaths are unexpected. Some are planned, some come by surprise and some are anticipated well in advance. Death can be painful, whether physically or emotionally, but it can also be beautiful, peaceful and quite rewarding.

Whether you're young, old or somewhere in-between, there will come a time when the option for more time is exhausted. If we know the end of life is near, we will find ourselves at a fork in the road: we can either choose to live our remaining days to their fullest, or essentially give in and allow ourselves to wither away mentally, emotionally and spiritually, long before we take that last breath.

This book is about choosing to live, and live well, regardless of the circum-stances. It's about moving to a place of acceptance and peace. It's about making every moment count and recognizing that life is precious, regardless of how much of it remains.

Whether we have been told we have just weeks or months to live, or we believe we have decades ahead of us still, there's no time to waste. The time to live well is *now*.

This book will discuss the beauty of turning a seemingly "nothing" into a "something," and making magic from even an ordinary daily event. Regardless of our own stories and limitations, we can choose to create a life that's truly worth living, even if our days are limited. Life is a delicate balance of sweet and sour, and we have the power to turn lemons into lemonade.

In these pages, you will read about my own end-of-life journey and my experience in dying a slow death from ALS. But that's only part of the story. Perhaps even more importantly, this book shares some of the lessons I've learned along the way – about how we react when we learn or suspect that time is becoming a limited resource.

My reaction: to really start living.

Chapter 1

The Diagnosis

The paint was layered thickly over the house exterior, its blue hue meek and muted – a mere shadow of the once-vibrant tone that had first dressed the bungalow back in the 30s. I envisioned a makeover that would transform the place into a Cape Cod-inspired cottage, and I swiftly moved forward with my plan.

A rich teak brown was more in line with the rock-laden exterior and would do the trick, I decided. I spent months painstakingly removing any shred of grass, replacing it instead with layers of rustic rocks, pavers and boulders. My efforts were paying off. I was slowly but surely turning this rundown bungalow into a blissful abode – a home that was beginning to resemble one I'd find on a postcard-perfect street in my favorite place in the world: Provincetown, Massachusetts.

Like any home, there were always things to touch up and finish. And wrapping up all the loose ends, however rewarding that may be, can be downright exhausting. That's precisely what I told myself one day as I put down the paint brush after just a half hour of touch-ups on the house. I was drained and the brush was heavy. My hand was giving out.

Odd for a bodybuilder, I thought. I even said to my partner, "Honey, I really used to be strong," a statement that was met with a light chuckle and the common "Oh, you're just getting older" retort. She then joked that jumping in to help was out of the question (she only carries a handbag and steers clear of activities that involve unnecessary lifting, bending or sweating, after all). I laughed, too, acknowledging that we each had our own jobs – and were good at them. Mine, to do the heavy lifting around the house; hers, to make sure I knew I was loved.

And heavy lifting I had done. Our home's rock exterior did not get there by accident. I had tackled it just two years prior to sprucing up the paint, and it was done without any pairs of paid hands. I laid those stones, one by one, some of them over a hundred pounds each. But now the small paint brush was heavy. I knew something was wrong, but I didn't know what. I had no name for it, no explanation. So I just went on ignoring it. I was a tough girl, after all.

That was July 2009. From then until the day I decided to go to the doctor, work kept me busy. I was reinventing my career, both within Memorial Hospital and outside it. I found myself working harder than ever, in part, because I had failed miserably at a new position, where I'd taken on an additional role (which just was not my forte) -- all while simultaneously managing the career I'd known and loved: running the hospital's surgical instrument and sterilization unit known as the Sterile Processing Department. Luckily, the hospital valued my work within the SPD and kept me on, assumedly because they saw my passion in that role and realized that, despite my best efforts, I couldn't succeed at everything. It was a good lesson for me. Not all things end in success, but some end in a few hearty laughs and an understanding that life can be messy. It may not always turn out the way we had expected or hoped, but it can still be good, nonetheless.

With my workplace challenges behind me, my ego healed, and a more balanced, less chaotic work schedule ahead, I began noticing other physical changes that I had ignored while my schedule was more hectic. By October 2010, I noticed more hand weakness. I was dropping things frequently and I knew that my "just ignore it" approach wasn't going to work much longer, especially since falling was also beginning to become a bit of a problem.

And that wasn't all. My voice had grown weaker and I could no longer jog up the stairs at work. In fact, breathing had become difficult, even at rest, and was outright labored with most movement or activity. I was also finding it difficult to chew and swallow some foods. Strangely, my muscles cramped horribly, too, twitching, stiffening and drawing tight like a Sailor's Knot beneath my skin. I could no longer hike or kayak and even daily chores were taking their toll. Exhaustion was my new norm. Something was very wrong and I knew I couldn't fix it on my own. So I saw a doctor.

After several misdiagnoses, a bout of respiratory failure and a stint in the ICU, I finally heard these words from three stern-looking Johns Hopkins physicians: *"You are not end-stage yet, but you have motor neuron disease."* Then, without another word, those doctors in their crisp white coats just got up, turned around and left the room. Paralyzed with disbelief, I just sat there stunned, my legs dangling off of the exam table.

After a few minutes, I got dressed and pulled myself together, knowing I had to appear brave for my partner, Johann, who was patiently waiting for me in the cold, unkempt waiting area. I remember being struck by the aesthetics of that little room – a place where impossibly difficult news was often shared with loved ones who had just spent agonizing minutes, even hours, sitting in uncomfortable, stained chairs, while wringing their hands and hoping for even a glimmer of good news. I remember thinking, *a waiting room should be better than this.*

Johann, a Registered Nurse, is a woman who, by exterior appearance, is impeccably pulled together and unmistakably professional. On the inside, though, is a gentle, kind-hearted, compassionate and, at times, fragile, individual who wears her heart on her sleeve and her fears on her face. Knowing her as I do, I pulled my emotions back in check, even tighter than they had been. I opened the exam room door and took a step toward the threshold. I glanced back quickly, taking in the cold, stark table still partially draped in a stiff white sheet on one end. Beside the exam table lay the bundle of technical nerve study cables and the machines that captured the involuntary twitching in my muscles – seemingly innocuous equipment that had just unequivocally told me and the doctors that my symptoms weren't *"just in my head."* That cold room told a story. It told *my* story and I already knew the ending without reading all the chapters. I walked out and this time didn't look back.

On my way back to find Johann, I saw one of the doctors in the hall. I bravely walked up to him and asked pointedly if I was going to die. "Yes, I'm sorry," he confirmed, matter-of-factly. He added that they would write a prescription for physical, occupational and speech therapies, but informed me that those interventions would only help make me more comfortable. His parting words left me hollow: "You'll need to go to an ALS clinic as soon as possible. They can give you a timeline and more information, and explain what to expect."

I left with Johann, in silence, my new cane in hand, and made my way to the car. Without my even saying a word, she already knew. She had seen the three doctors walk past the waiting room, and they had paused for a brief moment to look at her before straightening their lab coats and heading purposefully into my exam room. She had been in the medical business long enough to know the look of *"Okay, let's stick to the script. Be blunt, and be clear."*

As we headed toward home, it hit me: I was dying. Just 37 years young at the time, the thought of dying struck me hard, like a heavy rock upside the head. And then something else hit me...the realization that I now had to really start living. I didn't have time to waste.

Chapter 2

In Search of Acceptance

How do you learn to live, really live, when you thought you already were? What happens when you realize that you had the definition of *"living"* all wrong all of these years?

It dawned on me that I would have to create a new set of "living" parameters -- that the definition, the very language of the word "live," would need to become truly unique to me. No dictionary was going to help. The responsibility fell squarely on my own shoulders. Most importantly, I was about to embark upon not only a journey of a bodily death, but a path of uncovering the meaning of general social acceptance and inner peace.

I knew that this process was necessary, even if those around me, including those I loved most, hadn't yet accepted my fate and were unable to understand my acceptance and peace, and my willingness to look at life through a new, rosier lens. What a gift.

There are many definitions of the word *"acceptance."* For me, during the initial discovery of my terminal illness, acceptance meant one thing; and now, as I enter the "end stage" of my illness, it means another. Others may define it entirely differently. Acceptance is a unique and personal journey that truly cannot be bound by a simple, cut-and-dry definition or explanation.

Initially, I had to accept that the words from several different doctors, a couple of neurologists, some other physicians from different sub-specialties, and, ultimately, from a neurologist who specializes in ALS, were, in fact, the truth. At that point, acceptance meant recognizing that I indeed had this disease and was very sick.

Still, I had no real idea of what that meant. In fact, I soon began to understand that having that realization wasn't really acceptance at all. It was merely trusting that the doctors were accurate in their diagnoses, and that they had correctly identified my bodily limitations, the probable trajectory of my disease and the likely outcome.

At this point, it occurred to me that I might begin to be "lumped" into certain categories. I did not want to be, nor did I believe others in similar situations deserved to be, either. I decided I had to figure myself out – and quickly -- so I could begin discovering my own uniqueness, as well as of others who were also facing their own end-of-life circumstances. Only then, I concluded, could I live a life as fulfilling as I wanted and deserved.

I realized that to stay "me," the person I'd always known myself to be, that establishing this personal definition of "acceptance" would be critical. So began, in that very instant, the first of a three-part journey. My search to discover how to accept this diagnosis and prognosis, on my own terms, was beginning.

Although my journey toward accept-ance began shortly after my diagnosis, I want to point out that acceptance, by any definition, is not typically something that comes easily. My own would be no different. After all, part of acceptance lies in understanding the how, why, when, and where – everything about the circumstance at hand, really. And I had so much to learn.

Taking a long, hard and honest look at what harbors deep within oneself can be scary. It requires a willingness to allow whatever arises to hit you squarely in the face, and harder than any bad mirror day could do to an ego. It's not easy, either, when you are already feeling vulnerable and, at times, yielding to a situation or circumstance (in my case, a disease) that can take control, seize your mind, body and spirit, and hijack your mood for days, weeks or months on end. I knew, to my bones, that if I were to find any peace and create a path for living well that I would need to be strong now, during the initial phase of this devastating discovery.

My first post-diagnosis inclination was to spend some time alone (certainly not easy when you live with someone you enjoy, love to your core and feel an obligation to protect). So I decided to get behind the wheel, turning my passion for driving into a vehicle for self-discovery. After my work shift at the hospital, I'd just climb behind the wheel and go, first making a pit stop at Dunkin Donuts for a cup of coffee, my addiction. Then I'd be off, taking distant paths and various extended detours back to our home. I would find reasons to travel to the farthest shopping center. I spent a ton of money on gas, watched the mileage climb, and wasn't worried about it one bit.

At that time, I drove an SUV, a fantastic Tahoe. Oh, how I loved this thing! When I settled into that seat, I could see so much farther and wider than any other vehicle I'd ever owned. I felt on top of the world. I could see details along some the greatest country roads my small Pennsylvanian county had to offer – panoramic views that would have likely been missed had I been peering through a smaller windshield. Sure, I had seen these same views before I was diagnosed with ALS, but everything looked different now, more vibrant. On these drives, I was seeing life being lived all around me, almost as if I were seeing it for the first time.

Somehow, a gentleman whom I'd estimated was in his mid-seventies and whom I had seen at least a hundred different times perched atop his John Deere, suddenly looked different. He seemed more real, more *alive*. His worn straw hat told me he must be out in the hot sun often --that he needed to shield his likely balding head from scorching summer rays. His clothes were worn, too. I imagined he just slipped into any old pair of pants that morning, chowed down on some farm-fresh eggs and white toast, and then headed out, full-bellied, to work the land of his small farm. Maybe he was a widower or a weekend farmer who enjoyed the fresh air and the fruits of his labor. Maybe he didn't even own the property, but was working the land for a neighbor as a favor. I really had no idea about his story, but the point was I wanted to know.

I soon discovered that I wanted to know a lot more than just details about the old man I would occasionally see on my long rides home. I wanted to understand how and why things grew, and what caused those gorgeous trees lining up in the distance to just give up their breath and timber over on their weakest side. I wanted to understand why the obvious drug dealer down the street from our home could not see that he had other options, better ones. I suddenly found myself wanting to know why he hadn't embraced them.

With each day, I found myself wanting to learn and explore even more. I wanted to revisit everything I'd ever questioned. Everything around me, even things that I'd just noticed for the first time, had now piqued my interest. I suppose I wanted to be a part of life and not just watch it slip past me.

Along this journey, I discovered that life's choices were in abundance. I became keenly aware just how many opportunities we allow to pass us by in our lifetimes, and how many more are still out there just waiting for us to grab. This realization was both incredibly overwhelming and utterly fantastic.

In facing the fact that my life was ending, I wondered why I, and so many others, had made so many poor choices that impacted our lives. I pondered why some make better choices and choose a better path, even under the most challenging circumstances. This haunted me.

I began questioning whether I had truly tried hard enough. Had I lived by a fresher, if not better, set of standards? Had I done enough to help others? Had my life been significant and meaningful up to this point? Could I have or *should I have* done more?

All of this questioning and reflection served a valuable purpose. It helped me accept my new reality and begin making the most of my now-limited time. Whether or not all my questioning was reasonable or relevant didn't really matter. The very fact that these questions were on my mind made them important. And if I chose to ignore these personal and private observations, I would be ignoring the beautiful gift I was still given: life.

I am still alive at this point, I reminded myself. *So what am I going to do now?* If I could not figure this out, how was I going to live well for whatever time I had left? This was important for me because, up until that point in my life, I seemed to miss a lot of details, both large and small. I didn't want to repeat those same mistakes.

Again, getting to that point meant I'd need to discover the meaning of *"acceptance"* – both in a macro and micro sense. This would be the very first key to unlocking the box of answers on how I wanted to live, and how I could make that happen. Without it, I would be unable to see the state of my current existence and what made my life and all its various twists and turns different from anyone else's. And without that key I would have no effective gauge in which to measure and improve for the sake of myself and those around me who mattered most.

For 37 years I had believed that the word *"acceptance"* meant being okay with whatever situation arose. I adopted the notion that acceptance was this intangible thing that comes along with age or, rather, transpires at different stages of physical, spiritual and mental maturity. I now recognized that this was a rather shallow definition. Acceptance could be far more multifaceted, if we'd only allow it.

It wasn't that I was new to the concept of acceptance. Not unlike many people, I'd seen my share of tough times. I had witnessed firsthand a lack of tolerance and acceptance, beginning at an early age. As a gay, high-functioning autistic woman with little formal education, I was challenged to find acceptance as a person who didn't fit into the confines of societal norms. Labeled "odd" at a very young age, that seemed to shape my persona throughout life, even though I'd been considered knowledgeable and successful by others in my profession, and gained respect and recognition from my peers.

And now here I was, diagnosed with a terminal illness and labeled by my doctors as an ALS patient on borrowed time. This was the greatest obstacle I'd ever known. However much I welcomed my personal search for acceptance, I knew that this path would be the most difficult I'd ever traveled.

A 37-year-old gay autistic woman with a terminal illness. Of course, there's far more to me and my existence than that. I, like everyone else, have many layers – a depth that's been largely shaped by a series of life-altering events and experiences. My life, like anyone else's, is rich in detail and discovery. My life is certainly not perfect, but it's my own. And I wanted to continue living a life best suited to me, regardless of how much time I had left.

I wanted to right any wrongs, and chart a more positive, meaningful course. I wanted to learn and to really feel as though my actions, however small they appeared, were part of something bigger that would have a positive impact on someone or something. I felt compelled to put my value system to the test. Was this journey to self-discovery and acceptance important or necessary, particularly given my now-limited time? For me, the answer was a strong and unequivocal "Yes."

No doubt about it, life would be much easier if all our day-to-day circumstances, ideas, questions, and dilemmas could be addressed with a simple "yes" or "no" answer or black or white approach. Unfortunately, life doesn't work that way. We must uncover the "maybes" and the "grays" – that sweet middle spot or compromise. We must explore all of that and everything in-between that lies along the spectrum. It is here where we often find the true, honest answers we seek.

I also discovered that every point along this spectrum can and will change over time. How we felt yesterday or today may feel entirely different tomorrow.

And that's okay. Anger and despair can give way to hope and encouragement. And if we allow ourselves to slide in the other direction one day, that's fine, too. Living well doesn't mean you can't have setbacks or get mired down in a moment of negativity, sadness or anger. But we can find comfort in the fact that tomorrow is a new day. As long as we're here, we can choose to be here wholly and purposefully.

Without this understanding and acceptance, we become trapped in a place that leaves no wiggle room, and where we feel doomed by past experiences, outcomes, assumptions, and actions. We become limited in our ability to see that our *"norms"* can and often do change – and that we, too, must continue to change and evolve along with them. Change promotes self-growth, even if the circumstances that spurred the change are less than ideal. It's how we react to change that matters most.

Will we rise to the occasion when the chips are stacked against us, or will we fall like dominoes – each part of us caving under the weight and pressure? In my case, I found that my approaching "end" gave rise to an entirely new beginning. I couldn't necessarily change the way the story ended, but I could write all the pages in-between. I could live my life in grief, bitterness and despair, paralyzed by this disease and the fact that my life was being cut short, or I could pull myself up by my boot straps and start scripting some of my life's best chapters. My life's course had changed. This was my new reality, and I wanted to make the most of it.

You may wonder how you can focus on these "gray" areas of life, when death itself is on the farthest ("black," if you will) end of the spectrum. How, when we know death is coming soon, can we focus on living and finding joy in those final days? This isn't easy, especially when others, such as our loved ones and close friends, are involved and must also face the fact that death is inevitable. But we need to remember is that death is always coming, regardless of whether that news has come from the doctor's mouth or is felt deep within the soul. From the day we are born, we know our eventual passing is a certainty; what most of us don't know is how long we have. It really doesn't matter whether we are told we have five months or believe we have 50 more years – our goal should be to live well and, as cliché as it may sound, to live each day as if it's our last.

This is where things can get complex. A million questions might come to mind: *What do I (or we) do now? How will we choose to spend this time? What will happen from now until then (the end)? How will we navigate the challenges and new realities that present themselves on this physical, emotional and spiritual journey?*

When I was first faced with death, a million and one questions swirled in my head:

- *What is my illness going to look like -- now, tomorrow, a month or year from now?*
- *How will I physically change?*

- *What do I tell people? Should I stay silent or gather my support troops?*
- *Am I capable of handling this – whatever may come my way?*
- *What if I am not ready to go?*
- *How will I handle my loved ones' sadness? Will I be able to console them and keep myself from falling apart in the process?*
- *What about all of my unfinished goals and dreams?*
- *Can I handle knowing I might miss out on seeing my loved ones' personal life milestones?*
- *What if I am deserted?*
- *What do I do tomorrow – and how can I even plan for it when I don't know what each day will bring?*

These were scary questions, at first. No one wants to feel the shock of having to make major life-altering decisions "on a dime." Most of us need time to think things through and the best time for that is not when you've been smacked between the eyes with devastating or unexpected news.

While it's neither reasonable nor possible to plan out every remaining day, we can begin viewing life as a giver of both gifts and risks. From there, we can begin devising a game plan for handling what's next and living life well, even under the most challenging circumstances.

Indeed, there will be plenty of practical matters to deal with and manage along the way; however, the real challenge lies in the ability to balance all of this while ensuring that all of your personal needs are being met and that *living* remains the top priority.

Acceptance, I believe, involves the realization that death is the physical end for us all – and an understanding that life offers no guarantees. Not everyone will reach a ripe old age, an age that many might perceive as one well lived. It is possible to really live, and live well, even if our stay here is brief.

If we can live life from within a broader spectrum – where there's more to our story than just the black and the white

-- then we can begin to see the beauty in dying a slow death and living a life with meaning, joy and purpose every day.

Chapter 3

Redefining "Dying"

Along the way, we may also need to reevaluate our dialogue about death and our definition of "dying."

For most people, dying means a person is approaching the end of their physical life. We rarely talk about death and dying without intense emotion. In our culture, one could even say these discussions are taboo. Whether we're experiencing it ourselves or witnessing it with our loved ones, it's not easy. Many of us choose not to discuss it because those words make it real. We keep the topic at arm's length because if we can't put our arms around it, we believe it'll hurt less.

Clear and concise definitions help us navigate language in a more systematic, categorical way. Cut and dry, black and white. Our minds were created to categorize; this makes it easier for us to process information. It's a concept that is encouraged and cultivated from the time we enter school as young children, and it's perpetuated throughout adulthood. It helps us make sense of different groupings or topics. It helps to create common language for which general understanding becomes more possible. Unfortunately, it can also be very limiting, especially when we try to categorize death.

Death can be grim – but it can also be beautiful. Death can be scary -- or joyous. Death, or the process of dying, can be considered an end – or a beginning. Just as our own definition of "living" will differ, the same is true of "dying." If we choose to close our eyes to it and refuse to discuss it, we silently convey that death is "bad" and something to be feared. It doesn't have to be that way.

Whether we talk about death or try our best to sweep it under the rug, the end will still come. And there's no guarantee when the end will happen. Still, we are conditioned to expect a certain order to life – a list of milestones to occur before death comes knocking on our door. If it happens before then, it seems unnatural, especially cruel and somehow sadder than if it happens to someone who has lived what we would consider a long life. What I've learned, though, is that no death is more appropriate or inappropriate than another.

While it's understandable to want to live a long life and to feel heartache when a child or young adult passes "before their time," we can also appreciate that whatever time they and we have on this earth is precious and to be cherished.

I never expected that I would be preparing for my passing at this age. At the same time, I never expected that this very experience would be credited for helping me live life to its fullest, appreciating all the things, big and small, that each day has to offer.

I have found this journey to be a beautiful one, and I believe that if we could just begin talking about death and dying earlier we would be better prepared to focus on what really matters long before life's door begins to close. Perhaps this means teaching our young about the cycle of life a bit earlier, in an age-appropriate way, to help them waste less time and determine how they can best live in a way that honors their individuality and allows them to put their unique talents and goals to good use.

Imagine the possibilities that would unfold if we all started looking at the world a bit differently, seeing it as an endless pot of opportunities. Committing ourselves to looking wide and broad, thinking big, loving openly and honestly, being brave, and leaving a lasting impression – regardless of how many years or decades we are here -- would be one of our greatest gifts.

While each person will live, grieve and, yes, even die, differently, I believe a lot of good can come from keeping the lines of communication open, so we can share in the process and experience. This will foster acceptance and will make it easier to map out those next steps in the quest to live optimally.

Imagine the possibilities!

Chapter 4

A Personal Discovery

Usually, as adults we slowly evolve and believe we know who we are to the core. That can be the case for many people. Of course, there are times when we are faced with doubts and insecurities.

There are times when we wonder if we are on our right path. There are even times when we simply know something isn't quite right, but we are unable to label it. Worse yet, there are times when we are in a stagnating mode, simply going through the same motions, actions and activities day after day.

We may call it our "comfort zone," but if we were to be truly honest and privately challenge that idea, I suspect we might be craving more...of something. I know I was. And if I could just prepare myself mentally for this change, I knew this important transformation could begin.

No question, mental preparedness is one of the toughest parts of the dying process. Fortunately, it can also be one of the most rewarding. It can ignite and awaken parts of us that we never knew existed and even make us feel more *alive*. It is in this state of awareness when change is possible -- and when it can be attained with the least effort.

To me, being mentally prepared means some or most of your questions or concerns are either adequately answered or addressed. It could also mean that you have come to a place where no answer will suffice. Some might believe that this is where the entire preparedness process ends, but actually, it's just the beginning of one of the most beautiful legs of the journey.

Once your questions have reasonable answers or logical explanations, it frees your mind and allows more physical time and energy to be refocused on what will begin to matter most: living well.

Often, "living well" is just a synonym for "living differently." Getting there may require some additional preparation. Your body and, perhaps, even your mind, are undergoing a significant change. Notice, I refrained from suggesting both are in a state of decline, which, in my opinion, has a negative connotation. You are *changing*, and your new approach to living will need to match your new abilities and limitations, to at least some extent. This means that your head must be aligned with your goals, hopes, dreams, and even new realities.

How do you do this? Each of us will likely follow a different path in this process, although many of our steps might be similar. Here's what my process entailed:

Spending more time alone to think. Post-diagnosis, I questioned myself even more and some good, quiet "alone" time allowed me to work on getting my questions answered.

Setting new goals. Yes, I had goals prior to becoming sick, but I realized that many of them were no longer realistic. So I challenged myself to figure out what I really wanted to do *now* (and, interestingly, some goals that made my list were those I likely would not have believed were possible before). Writing this book was one of the personal goals I made for myself post-diagnosis.

Learning to be more patient.
Although life may begin to feel like sand sifting through open fingers, I worked hard to keep my fingers closed and grab hold of all life still had to offer. I realized that rushing through experiences just for the sake of completing them or being part of them would not cut it. I really tried to be in the moment. Being patient also meant recognizing that others, especially, my loved ones, may be slower in the acceptance process and couldn't be pushed to get where I was faster. I needed to remember that sometimes the person leaving grieves less than the one being left. I needed to allow the natural course to occur, realizing that the days, weeks or even months my

partner and other loved ones needed to come to terms with my "new reality," acceptance and desire to embrace life was a journey just as important as my own. This did not mean that I had to go it alone and put my own needs on the backburner in the interim; it just meant that I needed to be more reasonable, understanding and patient in my expectations.

Consciously seeing everything and everyone around me in a new way. We tend to rush through our days. With heavy work demands and family obligations it is easy miss opportunities to view things, *life*, in more meaningful ways. But slowing down to really discover and appreciate details of our day that might otherwise be overlooked – a kind word, the warm sun on your face, the rustle of the leaves under your feet, the joy of children's laughter – can bring pleasure to the most stressful, challenging or bleak day. It is possible to see life through a clearer, more focused and brighter lens. When I chose to use my eyes and other senses to "see" more, I could more easily overlook the pain of my condition and focus on more positive, joyful parts of my day. I challenge you to begin looking at life with a different set of eyes, too. Allow the disruptive noise and chatter that clutters your mind to fade into the distance. Focus on the things that appeal to you naturally, while also opening your mind to new details and experiences that might bring you joy and satisfaction.

Letting go of old, lingering resentments. We all have old wounds. In some cases, forgiveness has healed our wounds, allowing us to move forward in a positive way, no longer being held hostage by what hurt us. Sometimes, though, we go through our lives unwilling or unable to let go, allowing our wounds to stay fresh and painful. When I became sick, I knew there was no better time to let go of the pain, anger and resentment that still festered inside me. If I couldn't completely let it go or reconcile my past hurts, I at least worked toward finding a healthier balance that would let me come to better terms with the issue, person, or situation that had gnawed at me. Sometimes, stepping away from what hurts us or keeps us from living well is also necessary, even if it's painful at the time.

One of the most difficult moments for me was coming to the realization that I needed to release my sister from my life. It was a heart-wrenching decision. After all, who wouldn't want their sister by their side in a time of need or crisis – and, especially, when nearing the end of life? But I knew we had come to an impasse and that, despite my pleading to reach an amicable compromise, she was not going to budge and relinquish her set beliefs. It became apparent that nothing I could say or do would ever change that. And I needed to be okay with it. I decided that her unwillingness to bend, even the slightest, or even pay me a visit – despite her telling me she would – was likely her way of coping. I realized that she's only human and that, like me, wasn't perfect. We were different; we each had our own lives and they were far different. We grew apart because of a combination of real

events and unfortunate misunder-
standings. We went our separate ways
without ever giving one another the
opportunity to witness the growth we
had both experienced independently.
Now, I discovered, there was way too
much history – too much water under
the bridge – to bring us back together
in a meaningful, mutually beneficial
way. I no longer had the energy to try
and patch our problems and develop
an adult relationship with my sister. I
came to the conclusion that if our
relationship healed and blossomed
naturally, and she began looking at me
differently, on her own -- without being
pushed – that it would be a delightful
surprise. I would welcome it with open
arms. But I couldn't allow myself to
spend precious time, limited time,
waiting for something that might never
happen. Doing so would have
prevented me from living to my best
ability.

**Being more honest with myself and
others.** Pure, unadulterated honesty
takes practice. Most of us claim we do
not lie or convince ourselves that

"white lies" or fibs are harmless. But through this journey, I have come to learn that anything short of complete honesty and authenticity is harmful, especially for the person who's less than forthright. Often, we build these seemingly harmless barriers around ourselves or those we care about most. In doing so, we may shield them from the truth, whatever that may entail, to protect them from hurt, humiliation or pain. But at what cost?

Many can – and often do -- argue that the truth may be more painful than a softer, gentler version of it. While I certainly don't advocate verbalizing every painful truth or observation – or being honest to be hurtful -- I do believe it's important to really think about how our lies, however small they may seem, can impact us and those around us. I've learned that lies can create distance and damage the intimacy and legitimacy of our relationships.

You might be wondering whether we have a right to engage in full honesty, even if it means possibly shaping another's fate by the words we choose. That's not a question I can answer for everyone, but I personally found that I owed it to myself and those I cared about to tell the truth, share the facts and not mince words. And I wanted honesty in return. To me, honesty drives authenticity, and at this stage of my journey, especially, I was seeking a truly authentic life.

Freeing myself to be me. It's impossible to live well in the absence of knowing who we really are and the kind of person we were always meant to be. In our day to day lives, it's easy to assign labels to ourselves: *mother, sister, wife, husband, partner, nurse, teacher, homemaker, student.* But these are mere facets of who we are – certainly not the full picture. Digging deeper to really discover who we are and what makes us tick helps shape the next step in the journey, and allows us to lay the foundation for our next set of goals. When I came to terms with my diagnosis and prognosis, the fog began to lift and I could more clearly see the steps I needed to take to really be me and live the life I wanted to live.

Although I continued to work while I could – because it was my passion and was truly a part of who I was as a person – I no longer felt bound by professional obligations. It was up to me to break free of my once set-in-stone routines and become excited about what lay on the horizon. In doing so, I was able to more acutely tune in to the person I was wired to be. The weight of routine and everyday burdens and obligations naturally fell away. I began to see the shape of my authentic self being reflected in the mirror.

And I liked what I saw.

Chapter 5

Learning to Live

Learning to live may seem like a simple task, but it can be surprisingly complex. After all, haven't we been living from the day we were born?

Well, yes and no. Many of us have grown accustomed to blazing through our days, completing tasks and chores at Mach One speed, and following a routine, however comfortable or uncomfortable that routine may be. For years, a day in the "life" might have meant waking up, stumbling to the coffee pot, bleary-eyed and dazed, before jumping into another harried day of work, parenting, studying, cleaning, or what have you. How many times have we all said, "If I can only get through this day"? Make no mistake, being *alive* is not the same as *living*. And simply going through the motions of living is not living well.

Being happy may not be enough, either. Don't get me wrong – enjoying life and finding joy in each day is an essential component of living well. But even laughter and happiness can leave you empty if there's no real foundation to sustain it.

For me, living well meant devising a plan, a strategy for making the most of my days. I don't mean to convey that this is a rigid timeline that details what I must do every hour of the day. That's certainly not the case! Instead, it was about creating a loose, flexible framework of goals and dreams, and giving myself license to focus on things in life that brought me the most joy, made me think, allowed me to grow as a human being, and helped me feel more alive. It was about prioritizing what mattered most and letting some of the other daily clutter fall by the wayside. Again, it was about focusing on things that would allow me to be *me*.

Focusing on ourselves isn't easy. We're taught from an early age that we shouldn't be selfish. But often, our desire to not be selfish leads us to be downright self*less*. The very nature of selflessness – where we put everything and everyone ahead of ourselves and our own needs – prevents us from living well. I'm certainly not suggesting that we cease being empathetic and embrace a narcissistic lifestyle. On the contrary. For most of us, living well will involve building even more solid, meaningful and empathetic relationships with those around us. The message is that we can't lose ourselves in the process.

When embarking upon the living well journey, you may find that subtle changes begin to fall into place. When you begin focusing on more positive things – that delicious dinner before you, as opposed to the dishes piled in the sink, or the kind word you heard instead of the criticism – you begin to see life differently. And when we see life differently, we begin to live it differently.

In time, old habits of rushing through our day and checking things off our lists give way to new habits, where we slow down enough to appreciate all that the day has to offer. There will still be difficult days. Sometimes, you'll want to stay in bed and keep the covers pulled over your head (and you might decide to do just that). Some days will bring pain, others exhilaration. That's life. But we can choose to look beyond our moments of angst and despair, and appreciate that, regardless of that day's challenges, there are also gifts to be gleaned. And those gifts can come in all shapes, sizes and packages.

For me, one of my gifts came in the way of a heavy snowfall. Despite the fact that I now used a walker and had difficulty breathing, I found pure joy in pulling on my boots, slipping on my coat, grabbing a shovel and clearing a path from the sidewalk to our doorway. It was cold. The shovel and snow were heavy. And, for me, it was bliss! The fresh air, the weight of the shovel in my hands, the crunch of the snow underfoot, and even my bodily aches and pains, made me feel alive.

An early spring brought me equal satisfaction. The warmer-than-average temperatures, vividly green grass, birds chirping, gray clouds giving way to the warm sun. With each day, I paid close attention to the subtle nuances that made each day special. The scent of the coffee and the cup's warmth in my hand. The delight on my nieces' faces when they told me about their day. The pleasure of speaking with a faraway friend. The beauty in discovering something about my friends and loved ones (and even myself) that I hadn't known yesterday.

It's this reexamining and ongoing discovery that allows us to find pleasure in the most challenging of days. It's what helps reshape our longstanding belief system on what it means to live. It's what gives us the understanding that there's a significant difference in understanding and accepting an illness or condition, and learning how to really *live* with it.

When we are graced with this knowledge, we become better equipped to set our goals and plans for living well

into action, and start seeing positive
changes take shape.

Chapter 6

Putting the Past into Perspective

Admittedly, getting to this point in my life – where I was actively seeking all that was good, positive and pleasant about each day -- wasn't always easy or natural for me. And it certainly didn't happen overnight.

Not unlike others, my life largely revolved around a set of daily routines. I had a steady and rewarding profession and had earned the honorable distinction as an expert in the field of surgical instrumentation and sterilization. As such, I worked hard, logging long hours at the hospital and also from my home office. I served on various committees, wrote articles and developed educational programs. Pushing myself beyond the limits of "normal" workdays became my routine – and I didn't give it another thought.

I also had my routines around the house. In my free time, I'd putter around the house, repairing things, tidying the yard, grooming the garden.

I took pride in my home and my routines reflected that. Part of that, I reasoned, was because my home represented not only a physical address, but also my independence. I had purchased a home earlier than most, an accomplishment rooted in hard work and determination, and a need to become independent at an early age. My routines helped me care for this place, my brick-and-mortar symbol of independence and success.

My adult routines weren't determined by accident. Like anyone else's, they were shaped by my past – the trials, tribulations and triumphs I experienced through childhood, a difficult adolescence, and into adulthood. My life as I knew it was a byproduct of genes, environment and experiences, a menagerie of circumstances, education (and not necessarily the formal kind), and dreams.

My childhood and teen years were especially difficult. We had little money. I was often cold, thirsty and hungry.

My mother did her best, working multiple jobs to make ends meet, but her time away from home meant I was left in the hands of a harsh man. I didn't understand at the time that other kids my age didn't live like this – until I entered High School and saw huge differences in my classmates' home lives. It was the first time in my life that I saw the potential for options.

At first, I felt cheated. I wondered silently why my home and life wasn't like theirs. Over time, I began looking at the world a bit differently, carefully observing people and things, trying my best to figure out what made us so different – and what made me *me*. Was it financial status, race, education, and cultural differences that made us different and impacted the way we lived, or was it simply that some of us more clearly saw the options and opportunities, and made a concerted effort to attain them?

Until recently, I believed (or, at least, suspected) that people were either been born into a life that would naturally blossom into something bigger, greater or more meaningful, or born into the world of the lesser-haves, where there isn't much hope for a life too exceptional. For years, I didn't realize that every little aspect and detail of a person might influence the steps they take and how their lives are ultimately shaped.

Making amends with our past is necessary if we are to focus on our present and future. In rethinking our past, we must assess the "big picture" of our life's collective events. Only then can we balance the good with the bad, reconcile the challenges and struggles of our past, put unresolved (and, perhaps, damaging) issues behind us, and begin drafting a plan for living to our best ability moving forward.

Our past may shape us, but it doesn't define us. And it surely needn't limit us. We have options and we shouldn't wait to explore them.

I realize now that had I not had all my different experiences, including my difficult past, the way I approached life post-diagnosis might have been much different. I also realize that I may never have been able to write this book. I am grateful now for how I lived and for growing up in a rough-and-tumble neighborhood. I can also appreciate that the grade school bullying I endured played a key role in my developing kindness, compassion and respect for others. I now appreciate how struggling to learn *anything* until eighth grade has taught me that a long, arduous process needn't result in failure. I also have come to understand that the innocence I had lost as a child, and my being stripped of the freedom to just be me, made it all the more important for me to reclaim it now. There was no better time.

Those difficulties and disappointments have indeed shaped me, but they also allowed me to rise above the challenges of this journey. I have discovered that living well doesn't mean having all the answers on how to tackle each day bundled up in a neat, convenient and pretty little package. I've learned the value in being flexible, sometimes letting myself drift into foreign territory. I learned that a more panoramic, 360-degree view is often far better than a linear one. To live well, I learned that I'd need the freedom to explore. I wouldn't need to see over the mountain tops, just the path leading to them. And if I got lost along the way, I could simply chart a new course and try again.

Our past experiences and circumstances have given us the tools to chip away at life's challenges and find satisfaction and joy in some of the unlikeliest places.

I realized at age 37, while lying in a hospital bed, that I had a choice. I could grieve for a life that could have been and become bitter in the unfairness of having ALS, or I could start to see that all the events that led up to my diagnosis had given me the tools to cope with what was to come.

My hospital stay, with only my partner as a visitor after her long workday, left me with time to reflect. I used that time well. I tuned into the sounds of grieving families in the hallway outside my room. I noticed the harried pace of caregivers deciding which call button to answer first. At times, I reveled in my own silence and solitude in the midst of all the hospital chaos.

This time let me be free to reflect on my past and even forgive it – including any past hurts inflicted upon me by others. During this time of introspection, I recognized that people usually do the best they can in the moment, and that their best is sometimes in direct conflict with our needs and wishes at the time. If we seek acceptance for what was or is, we gain the power to rise above it.

Over the course of this personal discovery, I learned that the past was no longer my concern. I found that letting go and focusing on the present would help me live well and determine who I would become in the time that remained.

Forgiveness gave me freedom. And it felt wonderful.

Chapter 7

Overcoming our Limitations

It is often said that a persons' perception is their reality, and I believe this to be true.

It isn't so much how others perceive us, but how we perceive ourselves. If we see ourselves as incapable, weak or slow, or assign some other negative label, that will surely limit our ability to seek a more satisfying, full life. If we happen to be weak in body, we can still be strong in mind, will and spirit. Remember, the sum of our parts does not equal our whole.

That's not to say I didn't take issue with my own changing body and my new physical limitations. Just as many others experience, my body began to feel almost foreign, like some stubborn, uncooperative, nearly unrecognizable being all its own.

As adults, we typically don't just look in the mirror one day and wonder suddenly, *how did I become this*? Some may argue that this does happen to some people, but I happen to believe that through our lives, whether through subtle changes or bold moves, our self evolves and we actually do witness these changes, slowly (unless, of course, some life-altering injury or illness occurs and radical changes occur swiftly).

Still, a changing body can be hard to handle, and it's often even more difficult for our loved ones to watch. While we certainly will experience physical limitations, deficits and loss – as if our body is dying a slow death all its own – we need to reprogram ourselves to recognize that we can still do so much. Often, we just need to let go of the notion that living requires us to do all the same things we had done previously, and in all the same ways.

Reshaping your perspective on who you are, even in the presence of new limitations, takes guts. It may involve abandoning certain attributes that you or others once assigned to your name. But you can still be you. In my case, not being able to drive, rock climb, kayak, or even manage my department in the hospital made me no less me. Once I realized that, I was free to explore new avenues and cultivate new facets of myself, some of which I hadn't even known existed.

Now is the time to allow yourself to find new talents, hobbies and interests – or, uncover new ways of tackling some of the things that you don't want to relinquish from when you were your "earlier self." There's nothing wrong with compromising with our bodies, choosing this way over that in an effort to maintain our independence and stay aligned with the person we know ourselves to be. In fact, change can be both good and healthy. In some ways, it's not much different from learning to ride a bike for the first time...or leaving a marriage that is no longer working, or, perhaps, an employer whose goals no longer run parallel to your own.

What we might initially perceive as "losses" can actually be big gains. In the process of losing your label as the neighborhood's trusty handyman, for example, perhaps you are able to become a better friend to a lonely neighbor. Instead of lending a hammer, you can lend an ear. You can still remain *you*, just a new-and-improved version.

Allow yourself to take comfort in knowing that this new journey requires no map. Find solace in knowing that it's up to you to determine the destination. It just takes determination, perseverance and a strong internal compass to guide you.

Now is also a perfect time to play. Playfulness allows us to be open to new experiences and see that, sometimes, humor and laughter are our best weapons. Playfulness can pleasantly distract us and our loved ones long enough to stay connected to our true self – and shift the focus away from the fact that we are now this sick and dying person who used to do X, Y or Z.

I see most challenges as opportunities, and I challenge you to do the same. Yes, I get a lot of eye rolling with that recommendation, but I can assure you, positivity and sheer determination can work wonders on a spirit and keep you on the path to living well. The power of personal determination should never be underestimated or dismissed.

Tell yourself that the world is your oyster and you're bound to find the pearl.

Chapter 8

Fading into Peace

The goal of fading into peace is best not left to the days, hours or minutes immediately preceding our passing. How wonderful it would be if we naturally faded into a place of peace in the heart of our lives – and throughout our entire life cycle -- as opposed to trying desperately to find it when the end is near.

In my current terminal state, I find myself fading into a deeper place of tranquility and understanding. And it's happening as I am simultaneously living actively (and with purpose) and physically dying.

With this book, written with all the passion I could muster, at a time when hospice care is now my latest reality, I hope to lend comforting words for those of you who may be on a similar journey as my own. But that's not all. It's my sincere hope that these words will also help you live a better, more fulfilling life, regardless of your own circumstances – whether you are a caregiver or loved one of someone who is nearing the end, or merely a person who is still healthy and vibrant and seeking a better way to live *right now*.

No question, we have a better chance of living well if we focus on that goal before death and dying becomes an immediate issue. When this happens, our death-bed regrets become fewer and, hopefully, fade away altogether.

Fading into peace may mean letting go of our longstanding beliefs on what constitutes a rich, satisfying life. Instead of money, prestige and a cadre of creature comforts and material possessions, perhaps we should use love, kindness, compassion and our ability to share our gifts with others as our markers for success.

Fading into peace means slowly transitioning from one space or feeling into another, and relinquishing "what ifs" and regrets. Ultimately, fading into peace offers a satisfying, even welcomed, end to a great life journey.

Like virtually every other step along this journey, arriving at a place of unwavering peace will likely require some calculated and personal changes.

One such change might be creating a space all your own. "Space" can be associated with our immediate surroundings, such as home, workplace or other physical or tangible location that we might physically occupy. Perhaps even more significant, though, is finding a space within – a place that is truly untouchable and uniquely our own.

The concept of space is both personal and subjective. A single person living in a grand estate might feel suffocated, whereas, a person in a tiny one-bedroom apartment may feel anything but confined. Space transcends a place and often becomes more about a feeling than our physical surroundings.

When I speak of creating space, I am also referring to a process of shedding emotions that are no longer relevant or useful in your life. Letting go of people in your life who keep you down or don't allow you to grow will become more important now, as will releasing all of the things – actual or conceptual – that weigh on your shoulders.

If the space in which we live – home or heart – limits our ability to spread our wings and be free, it's time to reevaluate and, perhaps, move on (and by "move," I don't mean just moving your body, but growing your mind and soul).

Start making the necessary changes and expressing your needs and wishes now, not later. If you can't communicate verbally, recruit the help of someone who understands your wishes and can speak on your behalf.

Often, when we're the ones facing death, it becomes necessary to convey in a more direct way our wishes for the way we hope to live our remaining days. This is necessary because our loved ones often try, in good faith, to impose their ideas, suggestions and coping mechanisms on us. They mean to help, but when their wishes and desires conflict with our own it can be downright harmful.

If we are to gracefully enter any new stage in our life, it must be on our own terms. We deserve nothing less. We may not be in control of the physical changes we're experiencing or able to call the shots on how much time we have left, but we can and should decide how we want to spend it.

By giving ourselves the freedom and permission to create a bit of space around ourselves, we will be better equipped to stay focused on our own needs and wishes, and remain unclouded by others' thoughts, opinions and judgments, however well-intentioned they may be.

Just as we can create our own space, we also have the ability to control time. While we certainly can't add more hours to the day – or more days to our life, for that matter – we do have the power to control what we do in a day. Sure, there are those who work 60-plus hours a week, but there are still moments in-between that are ours to steal.

When I really started looking closely at my life, I was amazed at how much time I had wasted. By "wasting time," I do not mean when we consciously decide to take a break. Nor do I mean when we steal away for a night or weekend to get away from it all and abandon all our day-to-day responsibilities. I am talking about the bits of the day we lose unnecessarily, without gaining any satisfaction or benefit in return.

Not wasting time means making the most of our free minutes and available resources. It's about deliberately squeezing a bit more joy into our day and, in the process, getting more out of life. Not wasting time might even mean taking a brief nap or engaging in a fun activity that renews us and allows us to be more efficient in tackling more rewarding activities throughout the day. Perhaps that means baking your grandchild their favorite pie, massaging your partner's shoulders after a stressful day at work, taking a leisurely stroll or car ride with a loved one, learning that foreign language that's always intrigued you (even if it's just a few words to whisper to a loved one), reading "War and Peace," volunteering for your favorite charity or organization, or placing a note inside a bottle and sending it out to sea.

The choice is yours...and, regardless of our own unique circumstances, opportunity still awaits. Despite our limitations, we are still capable of living a purpose-driven life – one that gives our mind, spirit (and sometimes even our physical body) a bit of a boost, while, at the same time, allowing us to fade into peace.

Chapter 9

Leaving Your Mark

As I enter this end stage of ALS, now more than two years after my diagnosis, I am reminded daily how transformative this journey has been. I sometimes think back to that hour-long ride home from Johns Hopkins in April 2011 and revel in how far I have come.

Although my mind initially raced and my heart sank with the devastating news, I kept landing on two things: living well and remaining me. No question, I covered a lot of territory along this road. I've experienced loss, but have gained so much in return.

I've learned that life's journey doesn't have a set start and finish line. I've learned that even in the face of difficult discoveries and circumstances we can carve out a new and better path, one that leads to a better place and a better life than we could have ever imagined.

I've learned that we can become stronger in mind and spirit, even when our bodies can no longer keep pace. I've learned that when one door closes, we can still open another...and when we have to let go of some of the things we love, we can still grab hold of something else to help fill the void. I've learned that the things we gain are often more fulfilling than the things we've lost.

In my case, my inability to continue driving came on the heels of stepping down from a job I loved. I also acquired a feeding tube. All of these changes occurred over the course of just two months. In no time flat, it seemed, I went from climbing boulders and kayaking the ocean, to requiring a walker and wheelchair for even short distances. But even then, the game wasn't over for me. And it still isn't.

From the moment I knew that I – this athletic and active woman – would likely become bed-bound and die before 40, I began seeking something special. And I found it.

I've learned to accept and appreciate my own imperfections, as well as those in others. I discovered that when speaking became difficult, I could still write and engage with the world. I saw people through less biased eyes, and, with time, began seeing that they were doing the same for me.

Dying a slow death has given me time to become a better person, and the same can happen for us all. Life blesses us with daily opportunities to take a good look at our current paths, map out a new-and-improved plan, and begin searching for and becoming the person we were always meant to be.

I have no idea how much time I have left on this earth. But that's true for any of us. One thing I know for sure, though, is that I won't be wasting a minute of it. Neither should you.

Each day we're here, we still have a life to live – and a right and responsibility to live it well.

If we really open our eyes, we'll see that life is beautiful, and it's all around us. There are flowers to smell. Cool breezes to kiss our cheek. Wine to savor.

Smiles to capture. Eyes to explore.
Hands to hold. Loved ones to embrace.
Words to hear. Laughter to seek. Lives
to touch. Chapters to write. Above all,
there are dreams to dream and goals to
attain.

And when the book of life closes and we
draw our last breath, we can fade away
feeling truly fulfilled -- grateful for a life
lived well and for a glorious end to this
earthly journey.

How beautiful is that?

Afterword

Beauty is in the Eye of the Beholder:
A Caregiver's Perspective

The challenge of living with and loving Michele through this journey has been one of finding acceptance for me, as well. What we've each come to accept, and how we've approached our task has been fundamentally different. Michele's journey has been very tactical and cerebral. Mine has been emotional and laden with sorrow, spiritual angst, and thankfully, an occasional respite of humor.

A great teacher, Michele's lesson to me now is the same as it always has been. She will take me (literally or figuratively) to a mirror and show me what she sees. To her I am beautiful and perfect just the way I am – even when I'm "busy" steeped in the sorrow of anticipatory grief when she'd like to "really live" by taking a ride to see the water and get a Dunkin Donuts coffee. I am not yet (and may never be) at a place where I see the Beauty in her Slow Death. I have, however, accepted that it'll be here too soon no matter when it comes, and my soul will ache at the loss of the love of my life.

We have shared this journey together and I will continue right by her side. Already she's fading around the edges. It's okay,

because she's given me the best gift ever –
the awareness that she's lived a life of
purpose and has cleaned her slate in
preparation for whatever comes next. I've
watched her do it, and indeed, it is a thing
of Beauty.

~ Johann Becker

19987115R00045

Made in the USA
Charleston, SC
21 June 2013